The Art of Now

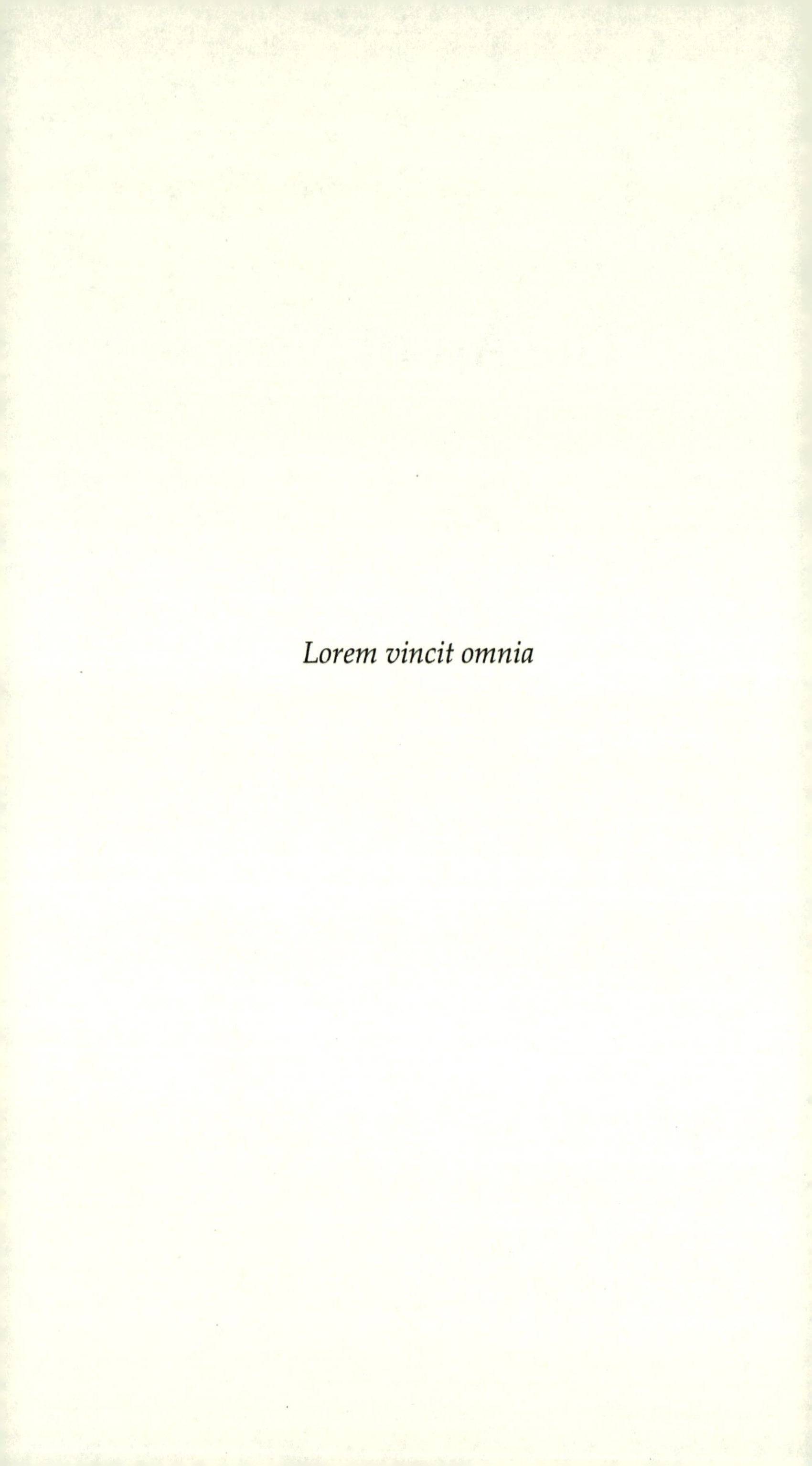

Lorem vincit omnia

The Art of Now

Creativity in the Present Moment

Tim Ljunggren

GENTLE THUG PUBLISHING

ISBN-10: 0-692-87639-1

ISBN-13: 978-0-692-87639-8

Gentle Thug Publishing

PRINTED IN THE UNITED STATES OF AMERICA

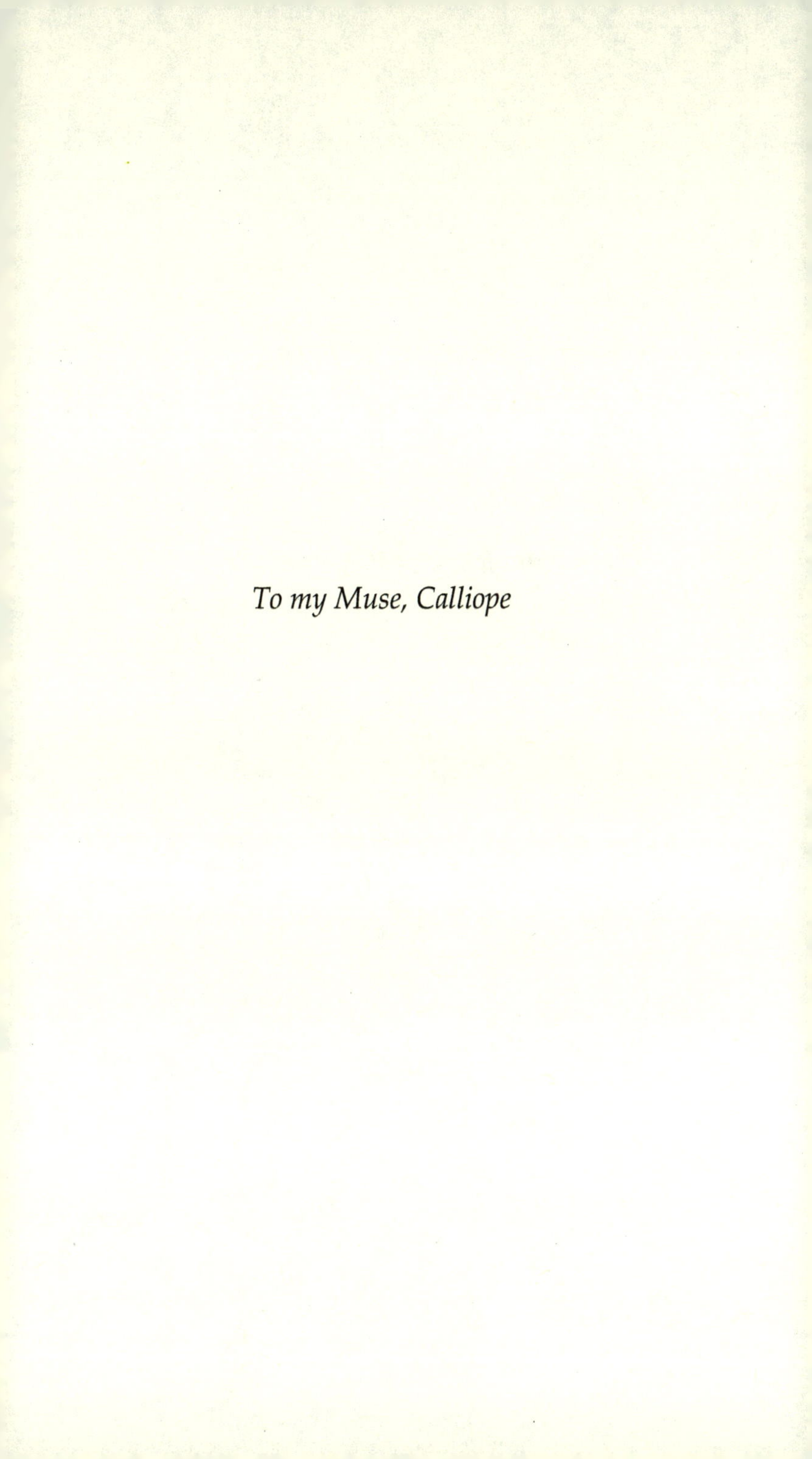

To my Muse, Calliope

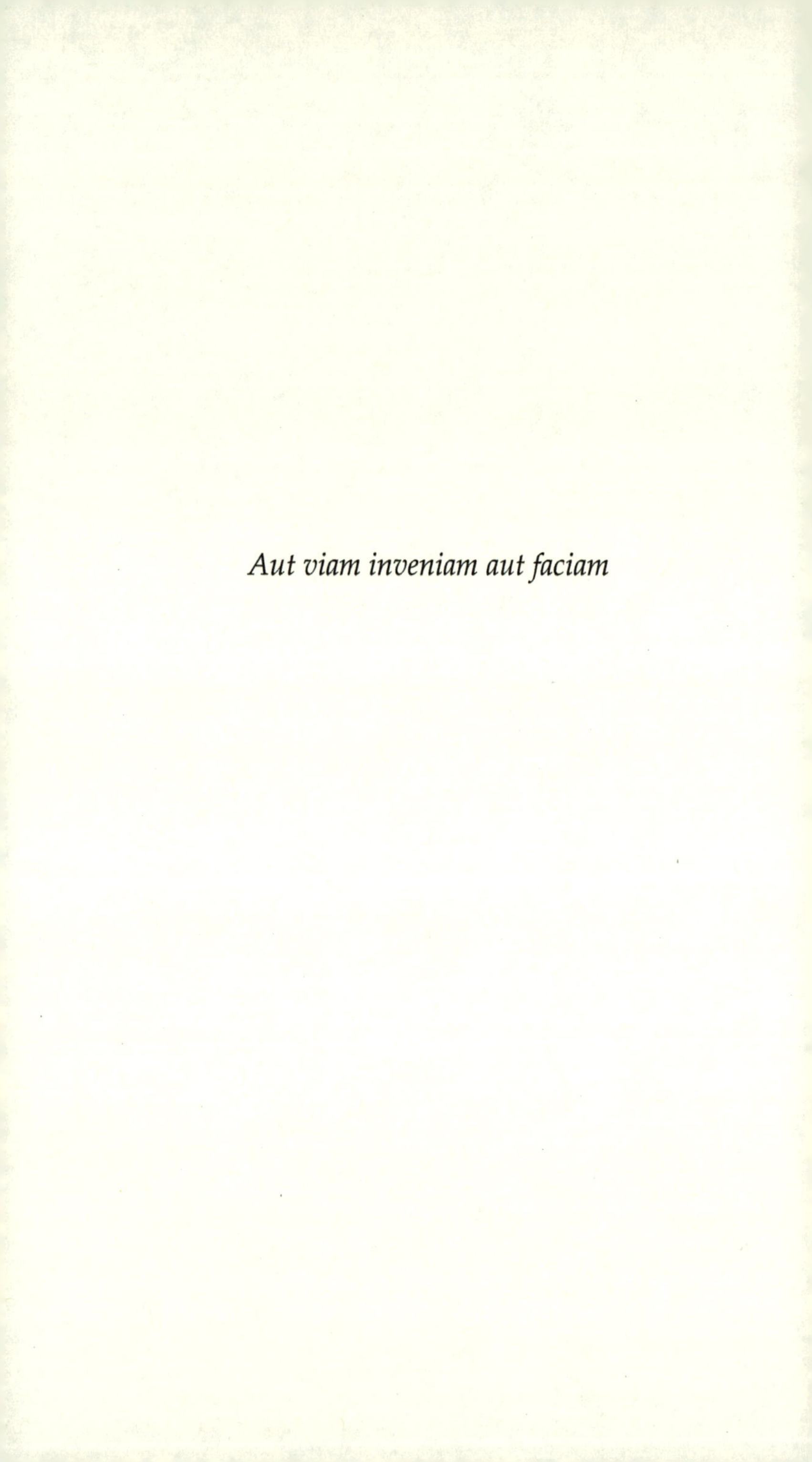

Aut viam inveniam aut faciam

Prologue: "I Am an Artist"—Coming Out of the Closet and Claiming Your Creative Birthright

"I am an artist. Any artist knows that their creations, their pieces must express an array of human emotion and experience. From the juvenile and innocent, to the erotic and the dangerous, and everything in between. Because Life is all of these things and more. It is the artist's divine purpose to reflect what Experience has shown them and others. What truly sets us apart from each other is whether or not we truly know ourselves enough to reflect objectively; but, through our own unique 'voice'."

- Solange nicole

"Do you want to know who you are? Don't ask. Act! Action will delineate and define you."

- Thomas Jefferson

Do me a favor. Right now, set down this book and find a mirror. Once you've found one, look in to it and gaze at yourself.

Then repeat the following words over and over again for one minute:

I am an artist.

Did you do it?

Chances are you didn't. *What kind of weird New Age crap is this?* you may have thought to yourself. *I've got better things to do with my time than to waste it looking at myself in a stupid mirror!*

If you *did* do what I asked you to do, how did you feel?

Did you feel embarrassed?

Did you feel like a fraud?

Did you feel exasperated?

Or, did you feel empowered?

To say, "I am an artist"—and to *believe* it for the very first time (or, for the very first time in a *long* time)—is the necessary pivotal step in becoming who you already are.

It's the recognition of your own powerful, creative force.

It's the acknowledgement of the vast artistic potential that lies deep inside of you, waiting for a moment to spring forth.

Waiting for *this* present moment.

As an artist and creative being, you can't afford to wait for the world to give you permission to do your work—or to step out of that cramped, darkened closet that has suffocated your creativity with fear and uncertainty for years.

You must claim your creative birthright and abide by your inner voice *now.*

You must choose to do your work *in this present moment.*

And the next time someone asks you who you are (or the next time you look in to a mirror), you can proclaim (without feeling embarrassed, fraudulent, or exasperated):

"I am an artist."

Fac opus tuum

Table of Contents

Prologue: "I Am an Artist"—Coming Out of the Closet and Claiming Your Creative Birthright....................................ix

Chapter 1: How to Start Being Creative *Now* (in *This* Present Moment).................3

Chapter 2: Listening to Your Inner Voice (While Getting Your Crayons Back in the Process)...17

Chapter 3: Mistaken Art (Or, How I Learned to Stop Worrying and Love My Imperfections)...27

Chapter 4: Gift Us with Your Creative Brilliance (Because the Rest of Us Need *All* the Inspiration We Can Get)............41

Chapter 5: Creative Risk Taking (Or, Getting to That Place Where Your F-14 Tomcat Can Fly Free)............................53

Chapter 6: Choosing a Major (or Two) and a Few Minors for Your Creative Work Will Keep You From Going Crazy...61

Chapter 7: "Not Now, Honey—I'm Not in the Mood" (Finding Ways to Get Your Work Done When You Don't Feel Like It)..71

Chapter 8: Picking Up the Pieces As You Go Along (Or, You Don't Need to Know

Where You're Going in Order to Get There)..83

Chapter 9: Using Your Inner Landscape for Your Outer Work (Or, Dream a Little Dream *for* Me)..93

Chapter 10: How to Deal with Criticism (Without Setting Yourself, and/or Others, on Fire).....................................105

Chapter 11: Keeping Up with the Joneses (Why Comparing Yourself to Others is a *Really* Bad Idea)....................................117

Chapter 12: The Art of Keeping Your Ego Out of Your Art............................129

Epilogue: *The Muse* (An Ode to You from Your Inner Voice)........................141

Additional Creative Resources............155

About the Author..................................171

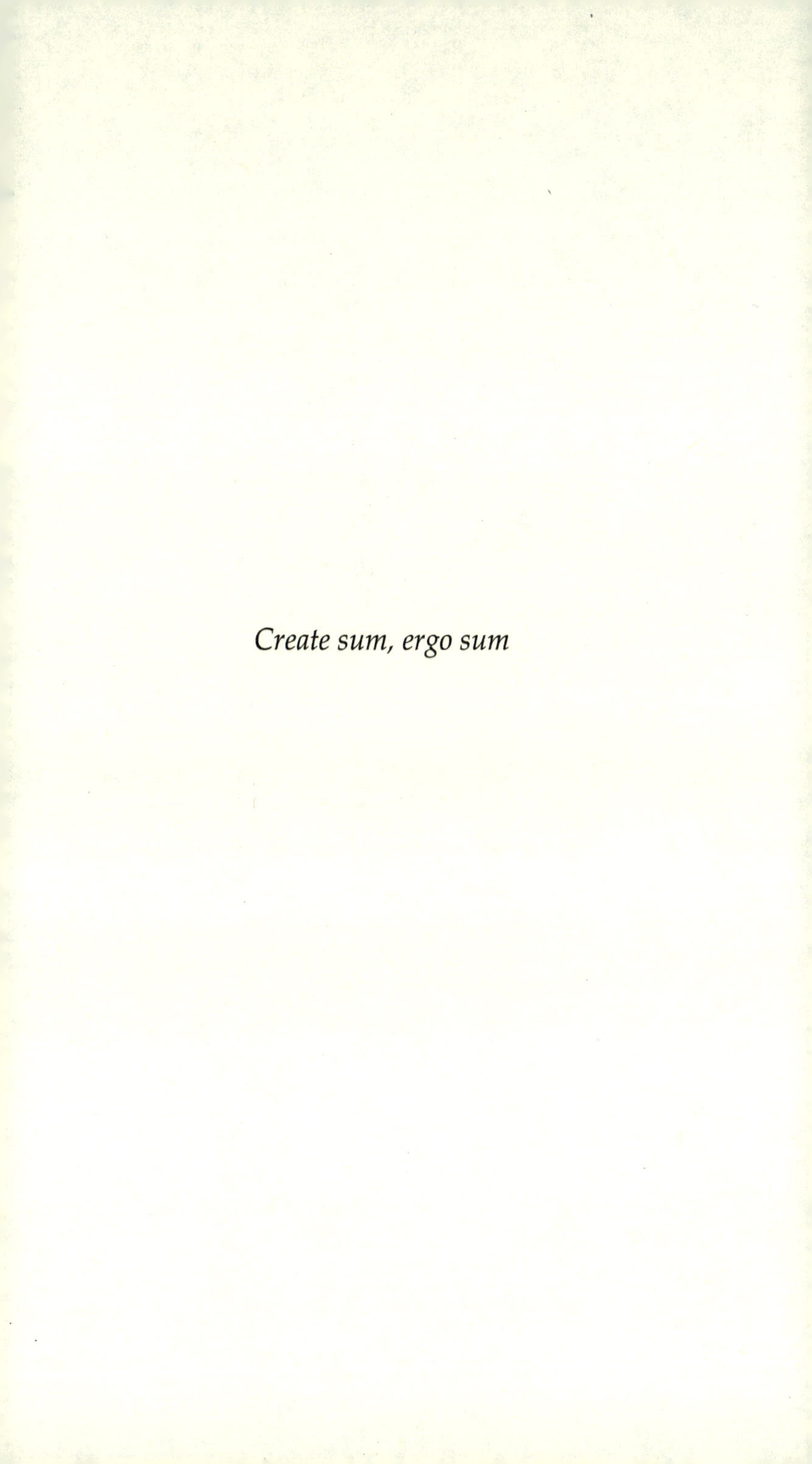

Create sum, ergo sum

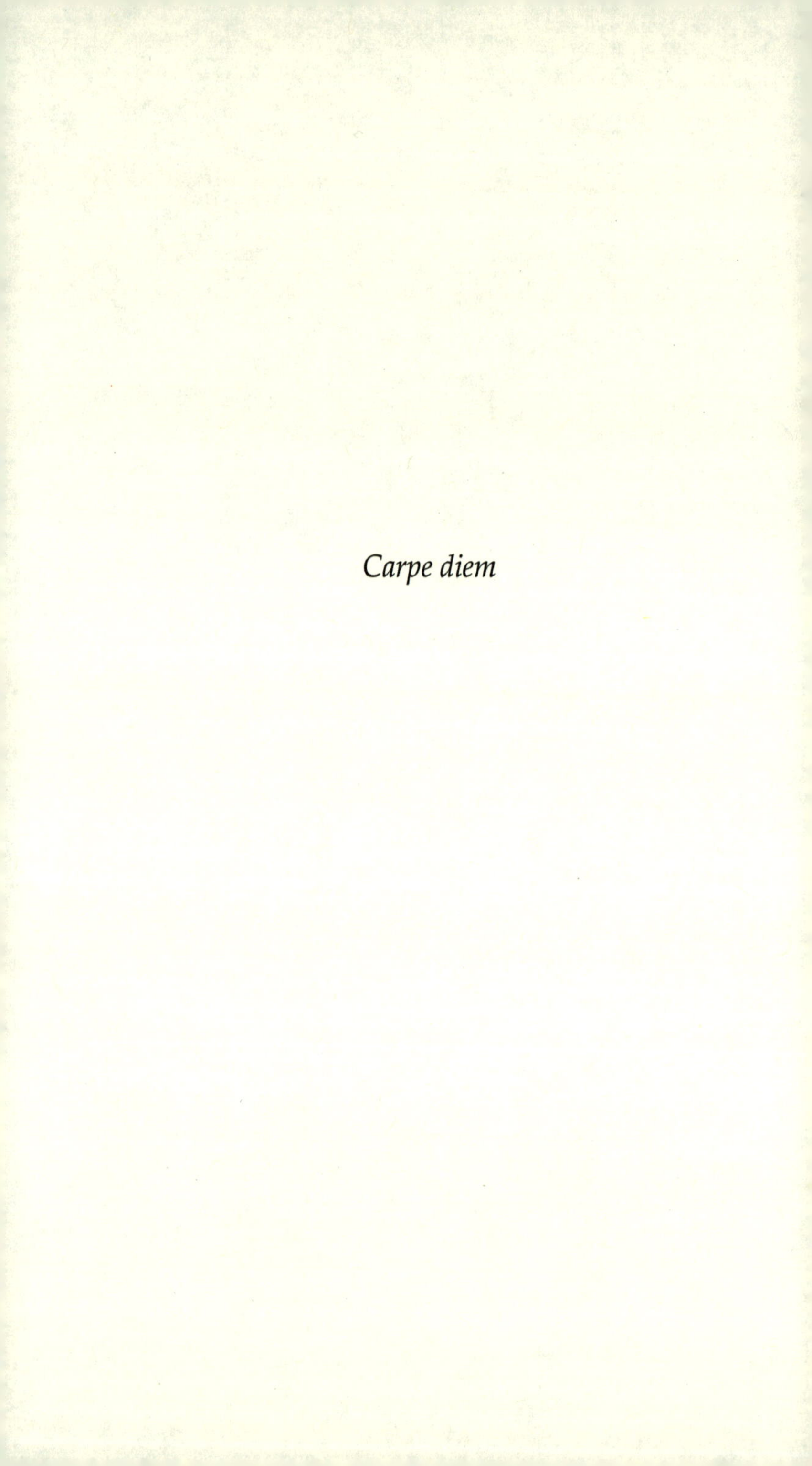

Carpe diem

The Art of Now

Creativity in the Present Moment

Una voce

Chapter 1: How to Start Being Creative *Now* (in *This* Present Moment)

"(...) Vivimos exclusivamente en el presente pues siempre y eternamente es el día de hoy -y el día de mañana será un hoy, la eternidad es el estado de las cosas en este momento."

- Clarice Lispector

"You must live in the present, launch yourself on every wave, find your eternity in each moment. Fools stand on their island of opportunities and look toward another land.

There is no other land; there is no other life but this."

- Henry David Thoreau

You have no tomorrow. You have no yesterday. All you have is *now*.

Right here--right now—as you read these words, your life is all about *this* moment in time.

No other moment matters.

For better or for worse. For richer or for poorer. Till death takes you away from this life and sweeps you into the next, your moment of clarity is right *here* and right *now*.

What are you going to do with *this* moment?

What are you going to do *now*?

As human beings, we're *all* creative beings. We yearn to have our inner voice heard through a multitude of artistic expressions.

We want to write novels.

We want to paint acrylic landscapes.

We want to be documentary filmmakers.

We want to be poets.

We want to be dancers.

We want to make the best chicken parmesan in the world.

What's stopping you in *this* moment?

What's stopping you *now*?

Our heritage of being artists and creative creatures is long, rich, and inviting. We're asked to embrace this immense history of human creativity (and beyond) by giving credence to our birthright as creative souls in the universe. It's our God(dess)-given right.

What's stopping you in *this* moment?

What's stopping you *now*?

Fear.

I truly believe that fear is the root emotion of all negative emotions that we experience and encounter in our lives as human beings.

Fear is the precursor of hatred.

Fear is the starting point of oppression.

Fear is the beginning of apathy.

And fear is what keeps us from doing our own creative work.

We want to write those steamy, passionate romance novels—but what would our parents say if we did?

We want to paint those acrylic landscapes of the Mojave Desert—but what would our significant others do if we took time away from them?

We want to direct a documentary film about the injustices of not being able to wear white after Labor Day—but what would the editors of *Vogue* think?

And what about that chicken parmesan that Grandma used to make (wouldn't it hurt her feelings if we tried to top her?)

Fear keeps us from using the present moment *now*. It makes us long for of how things used to be yesterday, and lures us into thinking that there will always be a tomorrow.

There's only *now*.

Fear sucks. Big time. Because it erases what we need to do *now* and replaces it with what we *should* have done in the past (which is impossible to recapture because we can't live in the past) and/or what we *should* be doing in the future (which is impossible to capture, because we haven't arrived there yet—the future is a present moment waiting to happen).

Stop doing that to yourself. You shouldn't *should* yourself. It's a very bad habit, and only leads to heartache and excessive binging on substances that aren't good for you.

All we have is *now*.

To help you start fighting against the ravages of fear—and to help you (re)start your creative process—I have two writing exercises that I'd like you to try (even if you don't consider yourself a writer, *please* do them anyway; the benefits you'll receive are guaranteed to boost your creativity and artistic well-being—or your money back).

The first exercise was introduced by Brenda Ueland in her book, *If You Want to Write: A Book about Art, Independence and Spirit,* which was first published in 1938 (Julia Cameron borrowed this same exercise from Ueland for her own book, *The Artist's Way*).

It involves keeping a daily diary.

This exercise is best done first thing in the morning, even before you have that nice, steaming cup of java (or whatever beverage you usually indulge in).

All you need is a notebook, a pen or pencil, and the willingness to commit to doing this exercise *every day*. Without fail.

The premise is simple—give yourself complete freedom to write down whatever random thoughts enter your mind, and write them down as fast as you can. Don't censor yourself and don't worry about grammar, sentence structure, or spelling (no one is going to read your diary except for you; your former high school English teacher is barred from perusing your entries).

Write at least three pages a day. Or more. (The more, the better.)

After you're done writing each day, don't read what you wrote. Stash your diary away in a safe place until the next morning. Every six months, you can *then* go back and read what you've previously written (but continue writing daily).

I know that this seems like a lot of work—but you'll eventually find some creative magic in your daily diary.

Trust me on this.

The second exercise that I'd like you to undertake is to write your obituary.

No, wait a second—write *two* obituaries for yourself. (Yeah, I know—this sounds incredibly macabre, but do it anyway.)

In the first one, write about what you'd be remembered for if you were to die *right now*—if you were to take your last breath this very second. Realistically look back on your life and ask yourself: What have I accomplished? What did I hope to accomplish? What did I want to become? What did I really want to do? Have I done it already? If not, why not? What disappointments did I have? What obstacles blocked me from doing the creative work that I've always wanted to do? (Were *you* an obstacle to *yourself*? Did you let others stymie your creative intentions?)

Put it all into words. Don't hold back.

In the second obituary, write about living to the ripe old age of 120—*without fear stopping you in your life*. You've accomplished everything that you set out to do. You were afraid of *nothing*—and that's reflected in your creative work and the rest of your life. You had everything that you needed at your disposal to be creative (time, money, freedom, etc.). What did you accomplish? What did you become? What did you do? What obstacles did you overcome?

(Did you tell Grandma to stuff her chicken parmesan recipe because yours is world famous? Did you proudly wear white after Labor Day and make a documentary film about it? Did your steamy, passionate novel make *Fifty Shades of Grey* read like a Dr. Seuss children's book? Did you run for a political office? Did you start a rock band? Did you open your own graphic arts studio? Did you do all those things, and more?)

Now compare the two obituaries.

Your first one may only be a shallow representation of who you really are, a shadow image of what you *truly* want to become in this life. It might be full of missed opportunities, failed realizations, and a straight-out denial of your own creative potential.

There's still time to change it.

Begin making your life a proud representation of your *second* obituary.

Start in *this* present moment.

Start right *now*.

Chapter 2: Listening to Your Inner Voice (While Getting Your Crayons Back in the Process)

"Artists strive to free this true and spontaneous self in their work. Creativity, meditation are ways of freeing an inner voice."

- Gloria Steinem

"Everyone is born creative; everyone is given a box of crayons in kindergarten. Then when you hit puberty they take away the crayons and replace them with dry, uninspiring books on algebra. history, etc. Being suddenly hit years later with the 'creative bug' is just a wee voice telling you, 'I'd like my crayons back, please.'"

- Hugh MacLeod

When we were children, we gladly welcomed and accepted the voice in our own heads.

You know which voice I'm talking about—it's was that inner voice that provided us with magical, mystical, and imaginative ways of thinking and interacting with ourselves and others.

It taught us how to be open to the abundant and free-flowing world of creative possibilities all around us and in us.

It led us on all sorts of incredible adventures, from racing our bicycle in the Daytona 500 to becoming an Olympic gold medal freestyle swimmer in our backyard wading pool.

It infused us with the notion that anything was possible, and that we we're capable of doing everything that we wanted to do.

It was the voice that only *we* could hear.

The voice urged us to color outside of the lines, to skip and dance to our favorite song, to draw and color pictures of birds in the backyard with our crayons, to be endlessly and effortlessly playful, inquisitive, and creative.

However, as we grew older, something happened.

We stopped listening.

We stopped believing.

That inner voice may have dimmed and may have been replaced by other voices—voices from parents, teachers, and/or other "authority" figures who truly had our best interests at heart.

We were taught to be responsible human beings—not misty-eyed dreamers who listened to "nonexistent" voices in our heads. We were taught to make respectable citizens out of ourselves, without giving a second thought to the crayon boxes and finger paints we were leaving behind. We were taught that "the arts" were nice to have around, but they couldn't possibly be as important as algebra and history.

We didn't listen to our inner voice anymore—we were too busy preparing ourselves for adulthood and all the grown-up responsibilities that were waiting for us down the road.

We abandoned something crucial in our lives in the hope of becoming what others convinced us we should become.

(There's that dreaded word again—*should*.)

But a funny thing happened on the way to adulthood—our inner voice never died. It remained deep within us, silenced for a while, yet fully alive. Patient, yet undeterred, it remained embedded in our souls.

Our inner voice waited for us. And waited. And waited.

And waited. ...

Maybe we were in our 30s or 40s when we reencountered that long-forgotten voice. Perhaps our lives weren't what we expected them to be and, in our restlessness, we began to uncover the voice that had been buried since our childhood.

Or, maybe we were in our 50s, 60s, 70s (or beyond) when we suddenly realized that we had far more yesterdays than tomorrows. In a panic, we may have been reminded of our childhood passions—and that singular voice in our heads—as they returned full-force and unstilled, coaxing, prodding, and cajoling us to become what we already are: Wonderfully creative beings.

Like Sleeping Beauty, our inner voice has been reanimated with a kiss—a kiss of our own remembrance.

That inner voice is back and wide awake now, casting aside its dormancy and offering us (once again) the possibility of a rich creative life to capture and explore.

And it has absolutely *no* intention of being put back to sleep again.

It won't allow itself to be ignored.

It won't allow itself to be silenced.

It won't allow itself to be neglected.

It won't allow itself to be maligned.

It has plans for us—big, scary, amazing plans that only *we* can accomplish.

Our inner voice is asking us to follow its lead.

Our inner voice is asking us to believe in ourselves.

Our inner voice is asking us to commit our lives to a creative existence, one that begs us to look at ourselves and our world in new and vibrant ways.

Our inner voice is asking us to live our lives free from fear, aligning ourselves with a creative presence that's both inside and outside of ourselves, urging us to recapture what we once lost or misplaced.

Our inner voice is asking us to pick up the pieces of our childhood dreams and desires, and to put them back together into a magnificent way of being and doing that will stir our imaginations and (re)open the doors to creative prowess.

Listen to your inner voice—what's it asking you to do *now* (this is excellent fodder for you daily diary entries).

Now might be an excellent time to find that box of crayons you left behind years ago.

Chapter 3: Mistaken Art (Or, How I Learned to Stop Worrying and Love My Imperfections)

"Have no fear of perfection—you'll never reach it."

- Salvador Dali

"We love the imperfect shapes in nature and in the works of art, look for an intentional error as a sign of the golden key and sincerity found in true mastery."

- Dejan Stojanovic

If you're anything like me (and I pray to whatever deity you're comfortable worshipping that you're not), you're a perfectionist.

You can't stand making mistakes.

Everything that you do—whether ironing the shirts, cutting the lawn, or doodling on a notepad—*must* come out *perfectly*.

Errors are the bane of your very existence.

Flaws are unacceptable.

Foibles drive you crazy.

Oh, you may be able to accept imperfections in other, lesser human beings—but you hold yourself to a *higher* standard.

Or, maybe you feel as if your only chance to measure up in the eye of your beholders is to become faultless, blameless, impeccable, pristine, unbroken—*perfect*.

I hate to break it to you, but perfection has *no* place in your life, and it certainly has *no* place in your creativity.

Perfection is the enemy.

Perfection is the devil incarnate. The bully in the schoolyard. The horrible, selfish ex that you were married to for almost 20 years. The monstrous ex-mother-in-law that almost destroyed your life for nearly two decades. (Not that I'm writing from personal experience or anything—I would *never* do that!).

As an artist and creative being, perfection will destroy both you and your work, if you let it.

Wait a minute, I can hear you saying, *does that mean I shouldn't care about what I paint, film, dance, write, cook, doodle, or whatever the hell else I'm doing (including ironing those shirts and cutting that lawn)? Does that mean it's perfectly acceptable for me to slop anything together and call it art?*

No. I'm not saying that at all.

When we do our creative work, we come to the work with our best intentions and efforts intact. We clear our minds and our hearts to create something unique, beautiful, vital, real, stunning, controversial, or whatever other adjective that you'd like to use.

When we do our creative work, we come to the work to have our inner voice heard.

Our relationship with our art is both personal and intimate. Just like any other relationship that we truly care about, we want to make it work for all the parties involved, and (hopefully) we want to become better human beings in the process.

But a relationship based on *fear* is no relationship at all.

Perfectionism is based on fear.

Fear that we're not measuring up.

Fear that we're lacking something.

Fear that our creative work will be scorned.

Fear that we'll never be as good as Andy Warhol, Lady Gaga, Maya Angelou, Gordon Ramsay, Meryl Streep, or Jay-Z.

Fear that we just can't cut it as artists and creative beings.

Fear that we'll be labeled as phonies or dilettantes.

So, in response to our fear, we turn to perfectionism as our savior—if we're perfect, we'll make "it" (whatever "it" is).

What we fail to realize is that, in our pursuit of perfection, we strangle ourselves by making *perfect* an art form rather than just sitting down and doing our real creative work. We get caught up in the minutiae of finding just the *right* word, just the *right* color, just the *right* camera angle, just the *right* dance move rather than relying on our inner voice (remember that?) to guide and inform us.

Allow me give you a personal example from my own perfect life.

As I wrote in my book *Koan Kreativity: Using Ancient Wisdom to Inspire Modern Creativity*:

> For years, I thought of myself as a filmmaker, but I rarely picked up a camera. It was far more important for me to keep my cup full by cramming it with books, lectures, and videos on the

techniques of filmmaking. How could I truly be a filmmaker without knowing the "rule of threes"? How could I call myself a filmmaker without viewing the entire film collection of David Lynch? And Martin Scorsese? And Jean-Luc Godard? And Alfred Hitchcock?

I was afraid to pick up a camera. I wanted to cram my mind with all sorts of filmmaking information and techniques to avoid picking up a camera.

I didn't want to be *just* a filmmaker—I wanted to be a *perfect* filmmaker.

That perfectionism stopped me cold and prevented me from doing the one thing that I needed to do the most to *become* a filmmaker: Simply picking up a damn camera and just start shooting.

Finally, one day, my own inner voice had enough of my perfectionism (fear)—it ordered me to go outside and shoot a video of my dogs playing in the backyard.

I balked. *Did Francis Ford Coppola shoot home movies of his dogs before directing* The Godfather?, I thought.

I was convinced that it was the stupidest, most time-wasting idea in the world.

Yet, my inner voice wouldn't leave me alone.

It kept nagging me.

Urging me.

Pushing me.

So, after much foot-dragging and gnashing of teeth, I finally relented.

I had planned to spend only three minutes in my backyard, but I ended up being there for over an hour. With camera in hand, I shot videos of my dogs doing what they do best—being dogs. They chased each other, fetched tennis balls, splashed in the kid's pool, and were utterly ecstatic to be the stars of an upcoming Hollywood blockbuster (in their minds).

The funny thing about it was that perfection never got in their way—or mine. They had no concerns about their running styles, their abilities to properly hold a tennis ball in their mouths, or their forms as they jumped into the pool.

They were having fun.

They were living in the present moment.

And so was I.

My camera and I zoomed, zigged, and zagged around the backyard in a frenzy. I got some great action shots of my furry friends (and a few *very* bad shots when I tied the camera to one of the dogs' collars for a canine's-eye-view of the action—he and the camera ended up running into the fence multiple times).

It wasn't a perfect filmmaking experience—but I had a perfectly wonderful time.

After that, I never hesitated to pick up a camera again.

(And, as an additional bonus, I got to revel in my friends' expressions when I told them that I had the best time ever shooting my dogs.)

My inner voice knew something that I didn't—creativity isn't about being perfect, but about finding new ways to express yourself through the world around you (and in you).

Creativity is about having fun—sometimes *serious* fun—and just letting go by doing the best you can in the present moment.

The trick is to drop all pretenses of perfection and create *now*.

Do me a favor—right *now* find a pen, a paint brush, a piano, or any other item that'll allow you to do some creative work.

Once you find it, use it for at least 30 minutes.

In fact, make it a point to use it as *imperfectly* as you can.

That's your *only* goal.

As I've already mentioned, the fear that hides behind perfectionism insists that our work be flawless every time we create something. This "it has to be perfect or why bother at all" approach to the creative process destroys the authenticity and uniqueness of our endeavors, and blinds us to the possibilities at hand.

Don't let it destroy yours.

Don't let it blind you.

Give us your *best* imperfections.

Chapter 4: Gift Us with Your Creative Brilliance (Because the Rest of Us Need *All* the Inspiration We Can Get)

"Creative work is not a selfish act or a bid for attention on the part of the actor. It's a gift to the world and every being in it. Don't cheat us of your contribution. Give us what you've got."

- Steven Pressfield

"You may not be a Picasso or Mozart but you don't have to be. Just create to create. Create to remind yourself you're still alive. Make stuff to inspire others to make something too. Create to learn a bit more about yourself."

- Frederick Terral

Believe it or not, but there are people in this world who're ashamed of their creative aspirations, dreams, and goals.

Are *you* one of them?

Guilt lays heavy on their shoulders. The perceived stigma of their artistic passions burdens their hearts. The daily responsibilities of "real life" dampens their creative souls and steals their ambitions, making them sheepish about living into their own creativity.

They continue to ignore that awakened inner voice of years ago that pleads with them to pick up a camera, a guitar, a crayon—*just pick up anything!*—and make some art.

They deny their very selves by not doing their creative work, and they deny the rest of us by keeping their inspirations and labors away from the world.

This is *not* a good thing. In fact, it's a *horrible* thing.

But there're good reasons behind this lack of faith in our creative selves and our artistic work.

Our society does an outstanding job in downplaying the importance of the creative process in general (and the arts in particular), so it's no wonder that people can feel both intimidated and guilty about pursuing their creative zeal.

For example, when school districts are short on cash and are looking for something to shave from the education budget, what usually goes?

Football?

I don't think so.

Music programs are usually cut. Photography programs are usually cut. Art appreciation programs are usually cut. Cooking classes are usually cut.

Another example of cost-cutting (some people would call it throat-cutting) maneuvering involves both our federal and state governments.

When money is deemed tight, it's the National Endowment of the Arts that gets smacked. The National Endowment for Humanities gets whacked. A slew of state-run, arts-related agencies find themselves on a hit list.

Yet, at the very same time that our society downplays the importance of creativity, it's also making tons of money off of it.

Want to know what several of the biggest industries in the United States are?

Film. Music. Television. Billions and billions of dollars are spent each year in our country on portions of our creative culture.

Want to know what several of the biggest exports from the United States are?

Film. Music. Television. Billions and billions of dollars are spent each year in other countries on portions of our creative culture.

Yet we still can't figure out ways to fund the band at our local high school.

How schizophrenic is *that*?

With all that in mind, you really can't blame people for feeling just a little bit ambivalent about their creative aspirations, dreams, and goals, can you?

Once again, you can't stop people from *fearing* the creative process (guilt, shame, ambivalence, apathy, intimidation, stigmatization, and many more negative elements are brought on by fear, whether self-induced, society-driven, or both).

And that's *exactly* why all of us need *you* to do your work.

Breaking the chains of fear—along with its many attachments—and doing your creative work is crucial not only to your own well-being, but to the well-being of those who bear witness to what you've brought into the world.

Finding ways to push through fear by writing the first draft of your book of poems, trying out for a role in a play at your local community theater, or picking up that dusty tenor sax that's been sitting in your garage for 15 years proves to the rest of us that it really *can* be done—and that we should *all* be trying to find our own ways to do it.

Our inner voice is sacred, and it's worthy of our *best* efforts—no matter where we find ourselves in our lives.

I know of a woman who, during an elementary school music class, was told by her teacher to "just mouth the words of the song, darling—don't try to sing them. You don't have the voice for it."

When I met her, she was 62 years old and had never opened her mouth to sing again after that incident in school.

But she *really* wanted to sing. She'd wanted to sing her entire life.

Finally facing her fear—and discounting the advice that her teacher gave her nearly 53 years prior—she took voice lessons.

Then she joined her church choir.

Then she joined her community symphonic choir.

Then she was chosen to perform a *solo* with her community symphonic choir.

She found the inspiration to do what she always wanted to do, and then she acted on it.

Say what you will, but *that's* the kind of inspiration that we *all* need.

Inspiration is about ordinary people accomplishing extraordinary things with their lives.

It's about *you* accomplishing extraordinary things with *your* life.

Inspiration is about facing the fear you might have and plowing right through it, allowing yourself to discover who you really are and what's important to you.

Inspiration is about being so filled with your creative spirit that it's impossible for you not to do your creative work.

Inspiration is about recognizing your own creative worth and letting nothing stand between you and your creative dreams.

What kind of inspiration will *you* gift us with?

What kind of inspiration do *you* want to share with the rest of the world?

What kind of inspiration begs to be released in *your* life—finding form or flavor—despite your elementary school teacher's (or some other appointed authority figure's) opinion of your creative self? (Or your own opinion of your creative self?)

What kind of inspiration will it take for you to allow *your* inner voice to sing at the top of your lungs? Or write your neo-Gothic satire novel series on current political trends? Or start your own photography business? Or produce your own podcast?

Only *you* can answer these questions.

Only *you* can inspire the rest of us.

Chapter 5: Creative Risk Taking (Or, Getting to That Place Where Your F-14 Tomcat Can Fly Free)

"This is our big chance to see what people think of us. The real us. We have to show 'em there's nothing to be afraid of. If we don't get over our fears, they never will."

- Lisa Harrison

"We avoid risks in life only to die, and end up facing the greatest risk which is having lived life risking nothing at all."

- Chinonye J. Chidolue

In the movie *Top Gun,* a young, cocky, hotshot Navy fighter pilot nicknamed Maverick (played by that affable Scientologist, Tom Cruise) is asked by one of his flight instructors why he performed a risky maneuver while flying a training sortie. "You don't have time to think up there," Maverick answers, "If you think, you're dead."

While Maverick was talking about the necessity of taking risks while hurtling through the sky at supersonic speeds in a F-14 Tomcat fighter jet (with a Russian MiG in hot pursuit), he could've just as well been talking about taking risks as part of the creative process.

As human beings, we long to keep things on an even keel.

We want to know what to expect today, tomorrow, next week, and next year.

We yearn to control all aspects of our lives, in the dim hope of creating a sense of safety and security.

The "status quo" of our lives is our comfort zones, and we may have a very difficult time giving up comfort for risk—for *not knowing* how things are going to turn out for us.

Yet again, we're talking about *fear*.

Creativity, on the other hand, *insists* that we take risks—both with ourselves and our work.

There is no "status quo"; each project that we undertake is different from the one before and demands that we utilize our intuition—our inner voice—rather than our rational thinking.

Otherwise, our creative work is dead or (at the very least) in a very serious vegetative state.

To keep our creativity alive and functioning, we may be required to do things we've never done before (or to do them in vastly different ways).

This can be either terrifying or exhilarating for us as artists and creative beings—maybe both.

Just like a fighter pilot, we don't know what we'll face when we take flight.

What obstacles will we encounter?

Will everything go smoothly, or will we hit turbulence?

Can we handle the rigors of completing our work when the work isn't going exactly the way we thought it would?

Are we able to chart a new course of action when things aren't viable for us anymore?

And what about that Russian MiG that's chasing us? (Or the obstinacy of a certain family member or friend?)

One of the biggest creative risk-takers of all time is the singer/songwriter Beyoncé.

Despite her massive success prior to 2013, she wanted to try something different. Tired of the "business as usual" attitude of the music industry, Beyoncé took flight in a very different direction.

And what a flight it was. ...

Secretly recording a "visual album" consisting of 14 song tracks and 17 music videos, her self-titled and self-produced enterprise was a huge gamble for her management company (which Beyoncé runs), not to mention her recording label.

With the help of Apple, Facebook, and Instagram (whom she secretly partnered with), Beyoncé released her new work at midnight on December 13, 2013—to the critical acclaim of nearly everyone on the planet while, simultaneously, turning the "status quo" of the music industry on its head.

She didn't do too bad financially, either.

Beyoncé's success and the risky methods she adopted to achieve that success were eventually used as a case study at the Harvard Business School.

Take *that,* Maverick. I'll fly with Beyoncé over you *any* day of the week, and *twice* on Sunday.

So, here it is, in a nutshell: Risk aversion is equal to creative aversion.

You can't avoid taking risks and be creative at the same time. The very nature of our creativity is founded on the principle of facing the fear of risking who we *think* we are and becoming who we *actually* are (which is reflected in the creative work that we do).

Pushing the creative envelope is a requirement in stretching and growing ourselves as artists; as uncomfortable as that may be at times, that's the only way our work is going to get done.

What risky creative behavior is stopping you right now?

What have you always wanted to try, but were too risk-averse to attempt?

If I could guarantee you the outcome that you desired in *any* artistic endeavor(s) you choose, which endeavor(s) *would* you choose?

Take a risk. Take more than one.

Expand yourself and your creative horizons by honoring that inner voice within you—it'll navigate you in the right direction.

Fly high, fly free, and fly *now*!

Chapter 6: Choosing a Major (or Two) and a Few Minors for Your Creative Work Will Keep You From Going Crazy

"What are the five products you want to focus on? Get rid of the rest, because they're dragging you down. They're turning you into Microsoft. They're causing you to turn out products that are adequate but not great."

- Steve Jobs

"Whenever you want to achieve something, keep your eyes open, concentrate and make sure you know exactly what it is you want. No one can hit their target with their eyes closed."

\- Paulo Coelho

As you're probably aware, colleges and universities usually require their students to pick "majors" and "minors" as part of their educational experience.

While being a source of pain, bewilderment, and suffering for many students, the practice of primarily focusing on specific areas of study (the "major"), coupled with a secondary focus on other fields of study (the "minor"), enables students to deepen their knowledge of—and skills in—whatever academics they may be interested in.

At least, that's how it's *supposed* to work in theory.

Unfortunately, it doesn't *always* work out that way in practice.

When I first started college, I initially majored in "Alcohol Consumption" and minored in two other areas: "Trying to Get a Date for Friday and Saturday Night" and "Recovering from My Major."

Obviously, my first attempt at college was *not* a stellar success.

Regardless of what you may think about the "major" and "minor" system of higher education, it serves a definite purpose: It really *does* focus the attention and effort of students on areas that they may be drawn to (if that attention and effort are applied correctly and earnestly by the students).

And that's why I'm suggesting that you adopt this system as part of your own creative process.

First, pick a "major" (or two, at the very most): What are you *most* passionate about? What does your inner voice want you to do right *now*?

Try to be as specific as possible.

Thinking about becoming a writer? Fiction or non-fiction? Poetry or short stories? Self-help or satire?

Does being a photographer tickle your fancy? Black and white or color images? Neo-realism or real life? Portraits or landscapes?

What about the graphic arts? Installation art or found objects? Masks or murals? Collages or graffiti?

How about filmmaking? Dramas or comedies? Short or feature-length films? Avant-garde or traditional storytelling?

You get the idea.

And, don't forget—you *always* have the option to change your major(s) if you find something that you're even *more* passionate about. In fact, many people begin with a certain creative focus which eventually leads them to *another* creative focus. So, don't despair if the major(s) you've chosen eventually give way to other forms of artistic expression.

Once you've chosen a major or two, go back and start the process again, this time focusing on other areas that may interest you—these are your "minors" (and I recommend that you pick two or three of them). If possible, try to choose areas that are different than your major(s).

Here's an example of my own "major(s)" and "minor(s)" list:

MAJOR(S)—Filmmaking (short films and documentaries) and writing (self-help books relating to the creative process).

MINOR(S)—Photography (black and white shots of people living their lives, along with landscapes), painting (acrylic neo-realism), and art media (digital art and design).

Once you've completed your own major(s) and minor(s) list, you'll have a literal creative smorgasbord to pursue. Your focus will become narrowed on what you really want to accomplish with your work.

But there's another benefit in creating a major(s) and minor(s) list that I like to call the "crossover effect."

Sometimes, we get stuck when we're working on a major project. Our creative juices seem to dry up and we're left hanging, wondering what we need to do next to finish our work (or, wondering if we'll ever finish our work at all).

This is the time to grab your minor(s) list.

By switching creative gears and working on something other than your major project, you keep your creativity flowing. Your mind is freed from the fear and anxiety of hitting that brick wall. And you're still *creating*—which leads to even more creativity in the form of problem-solving, insights, and other neat stuff which you can then use to kick-start your original project.

This worked for me while I was writing this book.

I found myself getting snagged about midway through, and came to a dead stop. I didn't know how to proceed—and it was driving me *crazy*.

Finally, I couldn't stand the craziness any longer and I broke out my trusty minor(s) list.

I chose "digital art and design," and spent a few days designing the cover of this book.

That's all I needed. I came back to writing with a fresh mind and with new ideas on how to proceed.

Yes, your "major(s)" and "minor(s)" list will keep you from going crazy—it'll also revitalize who you are as an artist (while, at the same time, giving your work (and you) a sense of balance, purpose, and direction).

Won't you give it the old college try?

Chapter 7: "Not Now, Honey—I'm Not in the Mood" (Finding Ways to Get Your Work Done When You Don't Feel Like It)

"Inspiration exists, but it has to find you working."

- Pablo Picasso

"Helped are those who create anything at all, for they shall relive the thrill of their own conception and realize a partnership in the creation of the Universe that keeps them responsible and cheerful."

- Alice Walker

It's been a rough day at your "real" job. You come home, exhausted, and find that your three-year-old came down with the flu. Not only that, but your significant other *also* came down with the flu.

Which probably means that *you'll* be coming down with the flu within the next 24 hours.

You need to get up early tomorrow for a big presentation with the boss. You have a ton of work that needs to be done around the house. Not only that, but it's April 14th and you *still* haven't started on your federal and state tax returns yet.

Oh, and by the way—did you forget about that mandatory parent/teacher conference tomorrow night?

Life seems to be coming at you full throttle, and it seems as if you don't have the energy to think, let alone do all the things that you need to do to live a productive and orderly life.

The *last* thing on your mind is to roll up your sleeves and do some of your creative work.

That inner voice of yours will just have to wait until tomorrow.

Or the day after tomorrow.

Or next week.

Or next month.

Or next year.

Or, it'll have to wait until after you retire.

God knows, you've tried in the past. You painted a decent watercolor portrait of your kids and the cat two or three months ago (and that left you feeling pretty good about yourself). You even managed to write a couple of short stories about the inane nuances of life, but that creative act took place over six months ago (or was it longer than that?).

But, right now, you're just not in the mood to do *anything* that's even remotely artistic or creative.

You're too busy.

You're too emotional.

You're too frazzled.

You're too distracted.

You're too fatigued.

You're too burned out.

You're too numb.

You simply don't have the time, and whatever time that you *do* have is devoted to other responsibilities and activities in your life.

You, kind ma'am or sir, are suffering from what I call Procrastinative Creativity Disorder (PCD).

The symptoms of PCD may include (but are not limited to) the following:

1. The inability to take seriously your creative dreams and goals.

2.. The ability to put everything ahead of your creative dreams and goals.

3. A muted disinterest in listening to your inner voice.

4. A sense that creativity really isn't *that* important in your life at this moment in time, or that your creative urges will be best served when you have more time (in the future).

5. The need to tell everyone that you meet how incredibly busy you are, and that you wish there were more than 24 hours in a day.

6. The inability to start, maintain, or finish a creative project.

7. An unhealthy interest in *Happy Days* reruns.

PCD is a serious creative disorder that requires immediate artistic intervention.

If you find that you exhibit even *one* of the symptoms listed above, it's imperative that you find the right motivation to get yourself back on track to becoming a highly functioning creative super hero who can leap tall buildings in a single bound (while doing your creative work in the process).

Creativity, like anything else in our lives that we deem important, requires prioritization and not procrastination. We need to get serious about finding the time necessary to hone our artistic skills and working on our creative projects.

Sure, it can be tough sometimes—but what worthwhile endeavor isn't?

Here are some tips to help you overcome PCD:

1. Realize that creativity is just as important as any other area or responsibility in your life.

2. Start a "creativity inventory" (which can be included as part of your daily diary) where you write down—each day—five ideas that you want to pursue as an artist (refer to your major(s) and minor(s) list that was discussed in the last chapter for extra help).

3. Scan newspapers, magazines, or internet resources for interesting tidbits, images, or stories that pique your creative interest.

4. Exercise—take a walk, ride a bike, go swimming, play racquetball, or do something else that's physical; there's a direct (and provable) correlation between endorphin release during exercise and creativity.

5. Set up a time and place each day where you can sit down (or stand up) and do your creative work. Even if you can't think of anything to create during this period, show up anyway—and stay there for the entire allotted time (at least 30 minutes per day at a minimum).

6. Collaborate with other creative people on projects that interest you.

7. Visit museums, attend concerts, frequent art galleries, and/or take yourself to other artistic venues that will invigorate your imagination, inspiration, and motivation.

8. Make a collage. Scour through old magazines and other periodicals, cut out pictures (or words) that capture your attention, and paste them on to a poster board. After you're finished, place the poster board in a place where you can see it every day.

9. Meditate each day for twenty minutes. Try and clear your mind as you simply sit still. Listen to your inner voice for

clues on how to proceed with your work, and how to overcome the challenges you may be facing.

These are just a few of my favorite things to help fight the insidious nature of PCD; being the creative genius that you are (and you *are*), I'm sure that you can think of even more items to add to the above list.

PCD is a manageable disease, but only if you put the time and effort into combating it.

And that time and effort is well worth it, believe me.

Don't let PCD become an epidemic in *your* life. Your creative life is much too important to let it simply slip by you without a concerted effort on your part to fully embrace it *now*.

Find ways (and the time) to allow yourself to do your work.

Chapter 8: Picking Up the Pieces As You Go Along (Or, You Don't Need to Know Where You're Going in Order to Get There)

"Some journeys take you farther from where you come from, but closer to where you belong."

- Ron Franscell

"Invention, strictly speaking, is little more than a new combination of those images which have been previously gathered and deposited in the memory; nothing can come from nothing."

- Sir Joshua Reynolds

Wouldn't it be just wonderful if we could envision our artistic projects from start to finish? All at once?

In a perfect world, there would be no sense of dread or confusion about what we're doing. Our creative vision for a project would be majestically laid out before us, complete with how-to instructions and roadmaps so we wouldn't get confused or lost along the way.

Everything would be clean, neat, and sterile, and we could start and finish our work with little or no trouble.

Welcome to the *real* world, kids.

At times, creativity can be a lot like watching a David Lynch movie: Baffling, infuriating, mysterious, beguiling, shocking, and taking us to places where we never expected to go.

There are no how-to instructions here. No roadmaps. Nothing clearly marked along our way.

Creativity is a tempter or temptress that beckons us with a "come and get me" wink, yet we're the ones left to figure out just how we're eventually going to capture it.

In a way, being creative is like being an investigative reporter—you're given bits and pieces of information about a story (or a project) that lead you further and further down a certain road (collecting other bits and pieces as you go) until you're finally able to put everything together into a coherent whole.

This sounds daunting, but it doesn't have to be.

Speaking of David Lynch again, it turns out that he's a master investigative reporter (along with being a gifted filmmaker); in his book on creativity entitled *Catching the Big Fish,* he echoes the importance of collecting creative scraps and putting them together as he moves along in his own work:

An idea is a thought. It's a thought that hold more than you think it does when you receive it. But in that first moment there is a spark. In a comic strip, if someone gets and idea, a lightbulb goes on. It happens in an instant, just as in life.

It would be great if the entire film came all at once. But it comes, for me, in fragments. The first fragment is like the Rosetta Stone. It's the piece of the puzzle that indicates the rest. It's a hopeful puzzle piece.

In [the movie] *Blue Velvet,* it was red lips, green lawns, and the song—Bobby Vinton's version of "Blue Velvet." The next thing was an ear lying in a field. And that was it.

> You fall in love with the idea first, that little tiny piece. And once you've got it, the rest will come in time.

It's not just Lynch who applies this approach to creativity.

For its advertising debut at the 2017 Academy Awards, Walmart decided to give four filmmakers (Antoine Fuqua and Marc Forster, along with partners Seth Rogen and Evan Goldberg) a chance to strut their creative stuff by supplying them with a random customer's receipt listing only six purchased items—bananas, paper towels, batteries, a scooter, wrapping paper, and a video baby monitor.

With just the receipt-in-hand—and nothing more—the filmmakers were tasked with making three 60-second short films that would be aired during the Academy Awards' telecast.

The "behind every receipt, there's a great story" campaign was a brilliant advertising move on the part of Walmart, and it was met with equally brilliant responses from the filmmakers.

Bananas Town (a musical-comedy directed by Rogen and Goldberg), *The Gift* (an out-of-this-world sci-fi extravaganza directed by Fuqua), and *Lost & Found* (a post-apocalyptic-themed little gem directed by Forster) all proved what could be accomplished when only the merest shreds of information are provided at any given moment in time.

Take note, fellow artists and creators of the world: Less is more.

Or, to be more precise: Less can *turn* into more, if we only allow our inner voice to guide us along that unmarked road.

The trick, of course, is to keep ourselves open, alert, and available to whatever comes our way.

As I wrote in my book *Koan Kreativity: Using Ancient Wisdom to Inspire Modern Creativity*:

> Creativity requires every-minute awareness., just as Zen does. From snatches of conversations that we

overhear in a coffee shop, to noticing the colors of the sunset reflected off our car's windshield, each moment brings with it the possibility of inspiration, while adding depth and meaning to our work—and our lives.

Each moment that you live brings you in contact with more and more creative pieces to collect; your task is to move forward, gather as many of these pieces as you can, and then arrange them in such a way as to stagger us with your ingenuity and creative spirit.

To help you accomplish this task, I recommend that you always carry with you a pocket notebook and/or your smartphone. That way, you can collect thoughts, words, images, and other pieces of your creative puzzles so that you can use them in your work.

Once you're gathered all those puzzle pieces in your notebook or smartphone, transfer them to a place where they're easily accessible to you. (For example, I've devised a cataloging system on my computer that I can easily access when the time comes for me to start putting my own puzzle pieces together.)

Believe me, you'll be glad that you did.

And your inner voice will be *so* proud of you.

Chapter 9: Using Your Inner Landscape for Your Outer Work (Or, Dream a Little Dream *for* Me)

"Dreams, my mother always told me, represent part of our unconsciousness--the place where we store the true parts of our soul, away from the rest of the world."

- Kailin Gow

"Dream when you are asleep...Make it true when you are awake..."

- Danya Krish

Do you know how the atomic structure of the molecule benzene was discovered?

Me neither. I had to look it up.

Apparently, a guy named August Kekulé (1829-1896) was a famous European chemist and whiz kid known for his work on molecular structures back in the 1850's.

He spent much of his time trying to figure out the arrangement of atoms in the benzene molecule.

This was a difficult and vexing problem because the ratio of carbon and hydrogen atoms that make up benzene was unlike that of any other chemical composition known at the time.

On one cold winter's evening in 1865, Kekulé had been working feverishly on the problem in his room. Totally exhausted and unable to find any reasonable solution, he finally called it a night, turned his chair toward the roaring fire in his fireplace, and fell asleep.

He began dreaming about atoms dancing in front of him; gradually the atoms arranged themselves into the shape of a snake.

Then, for some strange reason, the snake turned around and ate its own tail. The image of the snake—tail-in-mouth—continued to spin around and around in Kekulé's dreaming mind.

Suddenly, he woke up and realized what the dream was about: Benzene molecules were made up of *rings* of carbon atoms.

Problem solved.

When asked by his colleagues on how he discovered what makes benzene so unusual, Kekulé advised them: "Let us learn to dream, gentlemen, then perhaps we shall find the truth."

Whoa! If *that* story doesn't give you goosebumps, I don't know what will.

(Oh, by the way—serpents and snakes symbolize both fertility *and* creativity in many cultures.)

The tale of August Kekulé and his discovery led me to an incredible realization—there are forces beyond our control (and our rational minds) that can help us with our own creative endeavors (if we only let them).

These forces have a direct impact on our inner voice. And our dreams.

Kekulé's advice to his colleagues can also be applied to our own creative lives as well.

Dreams and creativity go hand-in-hand. Countless artists and creative people—from Salvador Dali (check out his famous hand-painted dream "photograph," *Persistence of Memory,* which helped to introduce the world to surrealism in the 1930s) to the Beatles (the melody for the song "Yesterday" came from a dream that Paul McCartney had)—have used their dreams to help propel their work, and there's no reason in the world why you can't do the same thing (and find your *own* creative truth in the process).

Not only can our dreams inspire our creativity, but they can tell us a little something about ourselves as well.

Allow me to share with you one of my own dreams that I had several years ago when I first started utilizing my creativity—while doubting it at the same time.

(Yes, my dream involved a snake, too. But it didn't involve benzene.)

One night, I dreamt that I walked into my living room and found a coiled, beige-colored cobra lying on the floor.

I was *terrified.*

I'm not a snake-person. In fact, I have a real phobia about these critters. I even look inside of the toilet—checking for snakes—before I even consider sitting down to use it.

Seriously. (That's how messed up I am.)

Anyway, back to my dream—

Although I was terrified to find a coiled, beige-colored cobra roosting on the floor of my living room, I *knew* that I had to get the thing out of my house, pronto.

So, I came up with a brilliant plan—I would throw a blanket over the beast and carry it outside.

As it turned out, this was *not* a brilliant plan.

In my attempt to cover the cobra with a blanket, it bit me—twice—on the palm of my right hand. My dream was so vivid that I could actually *feel* the sharp pain as the snake's fangs pierced my skin.

Now, I was *beyond* terrified.

The next scene of my dream found me running into an emergency room in a state of absolute, utter panic. I tried to explain to the receptionist that I was about to die a slow, horrible, and painful death because I'd been bitten by a venomous cobra.

I even showed her my hand.

She was not impressed and calmly asked me about what type of medical insurance I had.

What? I remember asking her incredulously. *Can't we talk about insurance later? I'm going to die a slow, horrible, and painful death!*

Nope. No deal. The receptionist calmly asked me again for my insurance carrier.

I finally told her.

She then politely informed me that I would have to pay my medical expenses upfront, and that my insurance carrier would reimburse me later.

That's when I woke up.

For two months, I tried to figure out the meaning of my dream, but to no avail.

It was like an obsession for me.

Finally, I approached a guy named Jon, who was a participant in one of the creativity clusters that I facilitated at the time, to get his take on the dream.

Jon was an expert dream interpreter; if anyone could make sense out of my crazy nighttime hallucination, it was him.

He listened carefully to what I had experienced and, after some very thoughtful consideration, he nailed it.

The coiled, beige-colored cobra was my own fledgling creativity (remember what serpents and snakes symbolize?). My attempt to cover up my creativity (and, ultimately, get rid of it) was met with a stern warning—this was something that

I was *not* supposed to do. My interaction with the emergency room receptionist was a reminder that I needed to rely on my own creative instincts by putting them upfront in my life, and not worry about how those instincts would turn out later.

I was blown away!

Not only by Jon's interpretation, but also by the fact that *something* was giving me hardcore advice on how to live into my own creativity by not shrinking from it (or trying to get rid of it).

I was dealt a doozy of a dream that got me back on track while, at the same time, allowing me to fully appreciate both my nighttime visions and my creative process.

Since that time, I've always made it a practice to keep a "dream journal" on my bed stand; it's simply a college-ruled notebook that I use to jot down dreams from the night before. The trick that I learned is to write them down within a minute after waking up, otherwise I'll lose them forever.

I strongly advise that you get into the habit of utilizing a dream journal as well.

As I've already mentioned, August Kekulé gave all of us some very sage advice when he said: "Let us learn to dream...then perhaps we shall find the truth."

Chapter 10: How to Deal with Criticism (Without Setting Yourself, and/or Others, on Fire)

"Criticism is just someone else's opinion. Even people who are experts in their fields are sometimes wrong. It is up to you to choose whether to believe some of it, none of it, or all of it. What you think is what counts."

- Rodolfo Costa

"I am my own biggest critic. Before anyone else has criticized me, I have already criticized myself. But for the rest of my life, I am going to be with me and I don't want to spend my life with someone who is always critical. So I am going to stop being my own critic. It's high time that I accept all the great things about me."

- C. JoyBell C.

In my book, *Koan Kreativity: Using Ancient Wisdom to Inspire Modern Creativity,* I included the following Zen koan (a philosophical riddle or tale) entitled "The First Principle":

When one goes to Obaku temple in Kyoto he sees carved over the gate the words "The First Principle". The letters are unusually large, and those who appreciate calligraphy always admire them as a masterpiece. They were drawn by Kosen two hundred years ago.

When the master drew them he did so on paper, from which the workmen made the large carving in wood. As Kosen sketched the letters, a bold pupil was with him who had made several gallons of ink for the calligraphy, and who never failed to criticize his master's work.

"That is not good," he told Kosen after his first effort.

"How is this one?"

"Poor. Worse than before," pronounced the pupil.

Kosen patiently wrote one sheet after another until eighty-four First Principles had accumulated, still without the approval of the pupil.

Then when the young man stepped outside for a few moments, Kosen thought: "Now this is my chance to escape his keen eye," and he wrote hurriedly, with a mind free from distraction: "The First Principle."

"A masterpiece," pronounced the pupil.

Kosen (the hero of the story) is a master calligrapher who's working on a major project; his assistant (the "bold pupil") attends to his master's needs, but can't help himself from constantly criticizing Kosen and his work-in-progress.

One interpretation of this koan is that the "bold pupil" is an actual person.

Another take on this story is that the "bold pupil" is really Kosen's own inner critic.

Either way, the main point of the tale is how to handle criticism (whether it's coming from outside or inside of ourselves) "with a mind free from distraction."

Kosen's response to the "bold pupil" and his constant criticism is simple and direct: He just keeps plugging along.

He doesn't argue, pout, or stop his work in frustration. He isn't unmanned by the sharp tongue of the "bold pupil."

Kosen literally keeps his focus on the task at hand and waits for the moment when the "bold pupil" leaves the scene so that he can continue his work uninterrupted and unencumbered.

And, after 85 attempts, he finally comes up with his masterpiece.

May we *all* be like Kosen.

Criticism (or the *fear* of criticism) has a special place in the collection of an artist's dreaded things. It can tear our creativity apart (if we let it) by leading us to despair, apathy, or defeat.

The wrong kind of criticism can pierce our creative hearts like nothing else.

Yet, whether misdirected criticism comes from a family member, a friend, an art critic—or our own minds—our job as artists and creative beings is to learn how to handle it while still getting our work done.

I should point out that not *all* criticism is bad.

There are two prevalent types.

Let's pretend that you write a short story and give it to me to read. After reading it, I say to you, "I really liked your story, but I think that it would be more effective if you used a first-person narrative rather than a third-person narrative."

This is an example of *non-toxic* criticism. You may not agree with my assessment of your work, but at least it gives you something to think about. And, who knows, maybe your story *would* be more effective with a first-person narrative (but, ultimately, that's up to *you* to decide).

However, if, after reading your story, I say to you, "don't give up your day job" and nothing else—well, that's an example of *toxic* criticism. There's *nothing* to think about—just a snarky negative comment meant to belittle or demean you and/or your efforts (whether intentionally or not).

Ultimately, *you* must decide if the criticism that you receive is valid or not. And you can usually tell the difference between non-toxic and toxic criticism by the way it makes you feel (after three or four days of receiving it).

As I wrote in *Koan Kreativity*:

Like Kosen, we're tasked with completing our own masterpieces. It may take us 85 times (or more) to get it "right," but each experience draws us into the next by enhancing our dexterity, understanding, and steadfastness.

Even more importantly, we're tasked with dealing with the criticisms that inevitably accompany our creative undertakings. Our ability to maintain a "mind free from distraction" is the key to our own artistic commitment and survival, and to maintain a reliance on ourselves as worthy and gifted inheritors of whatever our Muse may bequest us."

Here are a few more tips on the art of dealing with criticism:

1. Both non-toxic and toxic criticism can be painful. Acknowledge your feelings about the criticism you've received (a helpful and healthy way to do that is to write about your feelings in your daily diary).

2. Don't lash out at your critic. Regardless of the type of criticism you receive, simply thank your critic for her or his comments or don't say (or do) a thing. Work as hard as you can at not becoming defensive, demoralized, or demeaned.

3. Realize that different people are going to have different opinions about your creative work. Not all of those opinions will be what you expect (or want).

4. Maintain your creative power and authority to make your own decisions. Criticism can weaken your resolve to move forward with your artistic endeavors, so seek creative solutions to keep yourself in the game (working through some, or all, of the tips given earlier to combat PCD can be very helpful in this area).

Unfortunately, criticism may be a part of our creative process; try to take it in stride as much as possible, and allow yourself the time necessary to foster an ability to accept criticism at face value while (if it's appropriate to you) taking what's useful and applying it directly to your work.

Now, go and work on your masterpieces.

And don't let *anyone* get you down.

Chapter 11: Keeping Up with the Joneses (Why Comparing Yourself to Others is a *Really* Bad Idea)

"How much time he gains who does not look to see what his neighbour says or does or thinks, but only at what he does himself, to make it just and holy."

- Marcus Aurelius

"Whatever your passion is, keep doing it. Don't waste time chasing after success or comparing yourself to others. Every flower blooms at a different pace. Excel at doing what your passion is and only focus on perfecting it. Eventually people will see what you are great at doing, and if you are truly great, success will come chasing after you."

- Suzy Kassem

Your friend calls you on your cellphone, barely able to speak. She's beyond ecstatic, and you're the first person to hear her *fabulous* news.

"My film's been chosen to be shown at the Sundance Film Festival! I just got notified 15 minutes ago! Is that wild, or what?"

"Wow," you exclaim, barely concealing your seething animosity and jealousy, "how wonderful for you!"

Of course, *your* film *wasn't* chosen to be shown by those fine folks who run the Sundance Film Festival, even though you considered it to be *ten* times better than your friend's.

Actually, when you think more about it, your film was *twenty* times better than your friend's.

You're now seriously thinking about giving up filmmaking completely. Your friend's success has shattered your belief in yourself. and you feel that listening to your inner voice after all these years and finally doing your creative work was a huge mistake that has led you nowhere.

Stop it. Stop it right *now*.

Comparing yourself to others is a losing game that only ends in frustration, anger, envy, a sense of futility, and/or substance abuse.

You don't want *any* of those things in your creative life, do you?

Do you?

Look at it this way: There'll always be someone with artistic styles and creative abilities who's distinctly different from you.

Different—not *better*.

Comparing ourselves to others is a *hierarchical* thing—who's on top? Who's on the bottom? What can I do to make it to the next highest rung on the ladder? Who's a rung ahead of me?

We never ask ourselves where that ladder of comparison is leading us.

It's all about our egos (see the next chapter on those wonderful things called egos—they *deserve* a special word or two) and how we may feel the need to continually feed them by trying to be better than—or, at the very least, equal to—everyone else.

By contrast, the creative process needs to be viewed as a *communal* process—we learn from one another, our creativity is inspired by one another, and if someone attains something that we'd like to eventually attain for ourselves, that only proves that our goals are possible.

Comparing ourselves to others (and competing with them) has a long, flawed history in our lives—from early school memories of striving for the best grades, the funkiest hairstyles, and/or the cutest boy or girl in class, to more "adult" pursuits of striving for the next promotion at work, the second house in the Hamptons, and/or the cutest man or woman in the bar—which can lead us on the fruitless journey of having to better ourselves for the sake of keeping up with (or surpassing) the Joneses. Or the Smiths. Or the Kardashians. Or whoever else lives across the street from us (or resides in our own creative universes).

So, how do we stop this madness?

Joshua Becker, author of the bestselling book *The More of Less,* provides us with some handy-dandy ideas and methods to help us overcome the urge to compare ourselves and our work with others:

> **Become intimately aware of your own successes.**
>
> Whether you are a writer, musician, doctor, landscaper, mother, or student, you have a unique perspective backed by unique experiences and unique gifts. You have the capacity to love, serve, and contribute. You have everything you need to accomplish good in your little

section of the world. With that opportunity squarely in front of you, become intimately aware of your past successes. And find motivation in them to pursue more.

Pursue the greater things in life.

Some of the greatest treasures in this world are hidden from sight: love, humility, empathy, selflessness, generosity. Among these higher pursuits, there is no measurement. Desire them above everything else and remove yourself entirely from society's definition of success.

Compete less. Appreciate more.

There may be times when competition is appropriate, but life is not one of them. We have all been thrown together at this exact moment on this exact planet. And the sooner we stop competing against others to "win," the faster we can start working together to figure it out. The first and most important step in overcoming the habit of competition is to routinely *appreciate* and *compliment* the contribution of others.

Gratitude, gratitude, gratitude.

Gratitude always forces us to recognize the good things we already have in our world.

Remind yourself nobody is perfect.

While focusing on the negatives is rarely as helpful as focusing on the positives, there is important space to be found remembering that nobody is perfect and nobody is living a painless life. Triumph requires an obstacle to be overcome. And everybody is suffering through their own, whether you are close enough to know it or not.

Take a walk.

Next time you find yourself comparing yourself to others, get up and change your surroundings. Go for a walk—even if only to the other side of the room. Allow the change in your surroundings to prompt change in your thinking.

Find inspiration without comparison.

Comparing our lives with others is foolish. But finding inspiration and learning from others is entirely wise. Work hard to learn the difference.

Humbly ask questions of the people you admire or read biographies as inspiration. But if comparison is a consistent tendency in your life, notice which attitudes prompt positive change and which result in negative influence.

If you need to compare, compare with yourself.

We ought to strive to be the best possible versions of ourselves—not only for our own selves, but for the benefit and contribution we can offer to others. Work hard to take care of yourself physically, emotionally, and spiritually. Commit to growing a little bit each day. And learn to celebrate the little advancements you are making without comparing them to others.

In the end, comparison only leads to compromise—don't put yourself or your creativity into a compromising position by comparing either one to others.

Chapter 12: The Art of Keeping Your Ego Out of Your Art

"I equate ego with trying to figure everything out instead of going with the flow. That closes your heart and your mind to the person or situation that's right in front of you, and you miss so much."

- Pema Chodron

"Everyone always comes to one point in their life as an artist where you can either let your heart guide you or your ego."

- Louie Anderson

Answer this question as truthfully as you can: What's driving you to be creative?

Are you willing to try and follow wherever your inner voice leads you, or do you have some ulterior motives behind your drive?

Is your creative work one of the most important things in the world to you, or do you care more about your artistic reputation (or your future reputation?)

Do you want to do your work in the best way that you can and (possibly) find ways to share your creations with the rest of the world, or do you want to become world famous, make loads of money, have lots of groupies, and be on the cover of *Rolling Stone* magazine?

Be honest with yourself. ...

When I first started out reconnecting with my own inner voice and creativity, I was excited to see where the adventure would lead me. With wide-eyed innocence, I plunged into the artistic unknown with complete abandon, confident that something magical was about to happen.

And it did.

After about two months of religiously writing entries in my daily diary, a short story literally penned itself out of nowhere. The words flowed *through* me rather than *from* me. There was no conscious effort on my part, and there was no rational explanation to why this was happening.

It was as if I were some sort of conduit for a hidden alien presence that I never knew existed inside of me before (thoughts of the movie *Invasion of the Body Snatchers* flew through my mind).

Of course, the hidden alien presence was none other than my own inner voice.

After that first story came another. And then another. And still another.

I couldn't believe what was happening. The words to these stories just kept coming, forming themselves, unbidden, onto the pages of my daily diary.

I was in awe. As I mentioned, I was looking for something magical to happen, and I wasn't disappointed.

The reconnection with my own inner voice was more than magical, however.

It was a miracle.

Then I decided to see if I could get the stories published in several electronic literary journals that were floating around on the internet at that time.

I was in luck.

All three of the stories were eventually published, and I got to see my byline on every one of them.

After that, something changed. For the worse.

I got such an ego boost from seeing my own name in print that I wanted more of the same. It was like I took a hit of some exotic drug and got the highest high that I could ever possibly hope for.

I wanted to keep that high going (no matter what).

And *that* become my all-consuming obsession.

That incredible (and real) magic and miracle that I initially experienced were superseded by something else—something that was pretentious and artificial.

I stopped writing what my inner voice wanted to give me, and I started writing to simply see the words *By Tim Ljunggren* printed in a journal.

The magic disappeared. The miracle evaporated.

I had lost the purity of my inner voice by concentrating my efforts on becoming a "published writer" rather than simply doing what my inner voice was asking me to do.

My ego had become more important to me than my creative work.

I wanted to become world famous, make loads of money, have lots of groupies, and be on the cover of *Rolling Stone* magazine.

Obviously, I was in desperate need of some topnotch chiropractic care to get my creative center realigned.

I eventually stopped sending stories out to be published, simply because I got to the point of feeling miserable whenever I tried to match my writing to the style and taste of the editors who would be reviewing my stories for their publications.

In time, I begged forgiveness for abandoning my inner voice to stroke my ego, and I began to listen and follow again.

I concentrated on putting the work first, without regard to how it (or I) would be received. I returned to doing my work for one (and only one) reason: I had *no* choice.

The magic and miracle of creating slowly returned, and I refocused my energy on what mattered most to me—doing my creative work without obsessing over anything else.

Look, don't get me wrong—it would be *great* to become world famous, make loads of money, and be on the cover of *Rolling Stone* magazine (I left out the part about the groupies because I'm happily married to an incredible woman, and she'd kill me if I put the groupies back in my list).

But, if none of that happens, I don't really care—I just want to keep on listening to my inner voice and find ways to follow it, no matter where it leads me.

Creative success isn't dependent on how many literary journals publish your short stores, how many Tony Awards you have on your mantle, or how many art galleries hang your paintings.

Creative success comes from simply doing your work *now,* and then letting your work speak for itself. Whatever happens (or doesn't happen) after you release your work into the world needs to be an afterthought—not an all-consuming obsession that will drive you and your creativity into the ground.

Keep focused on what's *really* important.

Don't let your ego to stand in the way of your relationship with your inner voice.

Let your creative light shine regardless of where you find yourself, and let your work continue to inspire the rest of us to do our own work.

There can be no greater success than that.

Epilogue: *The Muse* (An Ode to You from Your Inner Voice)

You think that I have left your side...

That I no longer light upon your shoulder,

And whisper in your ear,

But you are wrong.

I am with you always...

For it is I who has chosen you,

To hear my voice.

Hearken to my words,

Your unbelief is not a barrier...

For I will make you believe again,

In yourself,

In me,

And in the Process that surrounds us both.

We are intertwined...

I am a part of you,

Just as you are a part of me,

For we are closer than lovers in a heated embrace.

I will never leave your side...

Nor ignore your complaints,

I will continue to shower you with gifts,

To show how much I care.

Feel me next to you...

Feel me inside of you,

As I feel you inside of me,

As you show the world the rhythms of your heart.

You are beautiful and worthy.

You are courageous and strong.

You are passionate and vigorous.

You are brilliantly creative.

You are mine...

And I will never leave your side,

My voice will become yours.

Set aside your restlessness and come back to me.

You will believe once again...

* * *

Taciturn invasions of the mind...

Quarried embezzlements of the heart...

Makeshift answers in silken sheets...

I spy,

I spy,

I spy...

A glimpse of the human condition,

Shattered dreams and hopeful sighs.

Allow me to introduce myself...

For the first time,

For the last time,

For all time.

* * *

Be not ashamed of your desires,

Or your passions.

For they are not meant to be cumbersome for you,

Nor are they meant to constrict.

They are the very essence of who you are,

And who you are becoming.

Embrace them as the night embraces the dawn,

And makes her its own.

* * *

You strive for perfection,

Which fells you every time.

Speak from your heart,

Speak from your soul,

Speak from your loins.

The warm presence of youth still present,

The clear manifestation that only age brings,

In perfect tandem.

Now is the time to follow your dreams,

Your desires,

Your Truth.

Speak to me,

My love.

Whisper in my ear.

Make me laugh,

Make me cry,

Make me burn with desire,

For you and your creative expression.

* * *

The healing power of creativity washes over you like the sun on a new day.

It caresses your soul with playfulness,

It embraces your mind with its tenderness.

Go deep.

Dive down under the surface,

Into the marauding depths of your creative nature.

You are protected and preserved by the glow of my love for you.

Do not despair.

Only believe.

* * *

You are bold.

Courageous.

An essence to be reckoned with.

A hawk circling far above,

With eyes on the earth below,

Missing nothing.

You see things,

That others do not see.

Simply because you are open,

To whatever I murmur to you.

* * *

You must avail yourself,

To the gifts that I give to you.

Do not blemish them by casting them off,

Or diminish them out of hand.

They are yours because you asked for them...

And I long to provide what you need...

Knock,

Knock,

Darling...

Please open the door...

* * *

Astonish me,

My love...

Embrace me with your passion and with your fire...

Do not turn away from me or your work,

Establish a true connection to both.

Believe,

Believe...

You are truly blessed by my presence and my ways...

Do not encase your heart in stone.

Continue to find me in the mundane,

The profane,

The sacred.

Open yourself to me as I long to open myself to you.

Astonish me,

My love...

Additional Creative Resources

Recommended Books

Creativity comes in various (and unique) forms, and so do the multitude of books written about the creative process; below is a selection of tomes that will enhance your own artistic tendencies:

The Artist's Way: A Spiritual Path to Higher Creativity, by Julia Cameron

The Mozart Effect, by Don Campbell

Creativity: Where the Divine and Human Meet, by Matthew Fox

The Mission of Art, by Alex Grey and Ken Wilbur

Better and Faster, by Jeremy Gutsche

On Writing, by Stephen King

Steal Like an Artist: 10 Things Nobody Told You About Being Creative, by Austin Kleon

Bird by Bird, by Anne Lamott

Koan Kreativity: Using Ancient Wisdom to Inspire Modern Creativity, by Tim Ljunggren

Catching the Big Fish: Meditation, Consciousness, and Creativity, by David Lynch

Fearless Creating, by Eric Maisel

The War of Art, by Steven Pressfield

Rebel Without a Crew, by Robert Rodriguez

The Creative Habit: Learn It and Use It for Life, by Twyla Tharp and Mark Reiter

The Writer's Journey, by Christopher Vogler

Recommended Films

Film is a wonderful medium to explore the creative process, and the following movies are just the things you need to open your creative universe to the passion of artistic pursuits:

Exit Through the Gift Shop, directed by Bansky

Beauty is Embarrassing, directed by Neil Berkeley

Big Eyes, directed by Tim Burton

What the Bleep Do We Know!?, directed by Betsy Chaase, Mark Vicente, and William Arntz

Shall We Dance?, directed by Peter Chelsom

The September Issue, directed by R.J. Cutler

Robert Selby Jr: It/ll Be Better Tomorrow, directed by Michael W. Dean

Steve Jobs, by David Fincher

The Social Network, directed by David Fincher

Take the Lead, directed by Liz Friedlander

Factotum, directed by Brent Hamer

Pollock, directed by Ed Harris

Daft Punk Unchained, directed by Hervé Martin-Delpierre

Short Films of David Lynch, directed by David Lynch

Moneyball, directed by Bennett Miller

Dangerous Minds, directed by John N. Smith

How to Draw a Bunny, directed by John W. Walter

Recommended Websites

There are a number of amazing websites dedicated to the creative process; here are several to get your creativity back on track (or keep it there):

Share a Story:

http://www.shareastory.org/

A place to try your hand at creative writing, along with other participants from the world over. Stories run from 1,000 to 1,400 words and cover a range of topics.

Creativity for Life:

http://creativityforlife.com/

Designed specifically for women (although men can probably learn a creative thing or two as well), this site is dedicated to turning creativity into an entrepreneurial art form.

TEDx:

https://www.ted.com/about/programs-initiatives/tedx-program

Creativity and innovation are the bywords for this impressive site. Guest speakers talk about how creativity has affected their own lives through video playlists, which will spark your own imagination and inspiration.

Speckboy:

https://speckyboy.com/

Geared towards web designers and photographers, this informative website provides great ideas and tutorials to help you along in your work.

Deviant Art:

http://www.deviantart.com/

Take a walk on the wild side where anyone can upload and share their art with a worldwide audience. You can get feedback on your projects from other members, and give feedback as well.

The National Endowment for the Arts:

https://www.arts.gov/

Their mission statement says it all: "The National Endowment for the Arts is an independent federal agency that funds, promotes, and strengthens the creative capacity of our communities by providing all Americans with diverse opportunities for arts participation."

Creative Bloq:

http://www.creativebloq.com/

Inspiration for graphic designers, illustrators, web designers, and other assorted artists, this site is a literal potpourri of creative information and advice.

Creative Allies:

https://creativeallies.com/

Want to create some art for your favorite rock star? Then this is the place for you—a gathering of over 125,000 creative artists who help in the branding process of musicians worldwide.

Brain Pickings:

https://www.brainpickings.org/

A website where creativity crosses the boundaries of art, science, design, and more.

American Zoetrope:

https://www.zoetrope.com/

Francis Ford Coppola's creativity portal where writers, filmmakers, and other artists share their work and improve their craft.

Academic Resources

Many colleges and universities have started the practice of offering no-cost courses online; you can tune-up your creativity by taking advantage of these wonderful opportunities!

Here are just a few examples:

The OpenCourseWare Project at the Massachusetts Institute of Technology (MIT):

https://ocw.mit.edu/index.htm

A permanent (and pioneering) MIT activity, the OpenCourseWare Project provides students from all over the world with web-based learning opportunities covering virtually all of its courses (including courses in the arts and mixed media, creative thinking and processes, and other related subjects).

The HarvardX Project at Harvard University:

https://www.edx.org/school/harvardx

Not to be outdone by MIT, Harvard offers its own free internet learning project; although not as comprehensive as MIT's robust course catalog, there are some interesting art and creativity-related classes available.

Stanford Online at Stanford University:

http://online.stanford.edu/

Stanford's online course offerings include everything from music appreciation to creative writing (and more).

OpenLearn at the Open University:

http://www.open.edu/openlearn/

From an introduction on how language affects creativity to learning how to find hidden meaning in photographs, you'll find some very interesting creative course offerings here.

About the Author

TIM LJUNGGREN is an Episcopal priest, a filmmaker, a writer, a mixed media artist, and a photographer. From 2001 until 2009, he edited and published the electronic magazine *Insolent Rudder,* which was chosen by *Poets & Writers* magazine as one of the top literary sites on the internet.

Ljunggren wrote and published the book *Koan Kreativity: Using Ancient Wisdom to Inspire Modern Creativity* in 2017, which focuses on Zen philosophy and the creative process. He is currently working on a feature-length documentary entitled *Big Sky Creativity: Montana Artists and*

Their Passions, along with other short film projects.

Ljunggren currently lives in Montana with his wife, Linda, and their three dogs (Cajun, Ranger, and Benji).

www.ingramcontent.com/pod-product-compliance
Lightning Source LLC
LaVergne TN
LVHW090943080826
845145LV00003B/871

* 9 7 8 0 6 9 2 8 7 6 3 9 8 *